DARK SYMPHONY

OMAVI WAITE

Dark Symphony
© 2010 Omavi Waite. All rights reserved.

No part of this book may be reproduced in any form or by any means, electronic, mechanical, digital, photocopying or recording, except for the inclusion in a review, without permission in writing from the publisher.

Published in the USA by:
The Deon Davis' Muteei Publishing Agency

Printed in the United States of America
ISBN 978-1-64467-398-0

Dedication:

to everyone who has ever dreamed.

Omavi

Table of Contents

Introduction 1
Dark Days 3
Blending Into the Sun 4
Drowning In Acid 5
Fade 6
In-Humane 7
Bookform 8
Braille 9
Beloved 10
The Demon 11
God's Adrift 12
The Exile 13
Poetic Orgasm 14
Skin 15
Overdream 16
Poetic Scar 17
Walls of Infinity 18
Serenity 19
The Mouth of the Void 20
The Great Dawn 21
Acknowledgements 23

Introduction

For in those dark days, I have seen images, rigid, horrid, encapsulated souls, left by misguided winds in the purgatory of time. Dark days, black raindrops fill the air, crack a stare, and recognize the solar flares. The deteriorating skies, black clouds and acid rain.

Dark Days

I feel that in those dark days, black raindrops fill the air around me. Evaporated sense of self, my sanity dried up as those black rain drops evaporate, turned to rock, my mind is as hard as stone, molded and smoothed, down to the bone, buried in a sense of evaporated self. I can't grasp who I am; only fragments and figments of my dripping imagination imagine my nation with the imagination of my images stamped on the doors of every nation. If you could see my vision and feel my inspiration when my blood boils at 30,000 degrees of inspiration, my vocal ability will mimic a supersonic rocket catching the debris of an atomic explosion. Poetic collision and mental implosions overdosed on potent doses of liquid formed images. Imaginary water colors smoothing out my reality you find my smothered vision smeared on my face. When I look to the stars and mentally project myself on mars, hopefully while I'm here I can make you feel the warmth of my solar bars.

Blending Into the Sun

Blending into the sun, traversing the universe, I feel destiny rising at my feet. My love for you runs so deep, you can find traces of my frequency trapped between the water drops of the Nile River, flowing forever into your stream of love and wisdom, you being my beacon of light reaching stardom sitting on mars. Let's go to the galactic library, and make love to the librarian, that would be oh so sweet, which would stimulate the mental arteries of your spiritual being electrolyzing the orgasmic spark of your channeling frequency. Dance in my mind with the way your mindset shapes the curves of your body I want to make love to your awareness, to your consciousness, if I could somehow detach myself from physical form and just become the air you breath, around you, if I can become your perception, if I could just make love to your consciousness with my awareness distorting fabrications of reality itself.

Overlapping universes our love will be so potent words wouldn't even describe how much we would stop all matter from vibrating. Come with me as we travel to the sun, in unison, as we become a number one.

Drowning In Acid

I am drowning in acid, dripping from my pours, clotting my circuits and breaching the normal flow.

Chrome liquid hardening on my skin I am being swallowed up by these acid words, burning my flesh each time I write a word, dripping my skin off forming word puddles on the ground. Trying to break free from this liquid bondage of these silver colored words fusing in my skin by the second seeping into my insides, drowning on the inside and burning on the outside my skin is fusing into this liquid silver acid burning everything on my body, chocking from this acidic liquid consuming my mind molding this acid turning my brain into this iron shell, that leaks words that leave 30,000 degree scars on my sensitive skin. I am drowning in words, I am burning in skin, and I am, these acid words.

Fade

A grazing essence from the creeds of man I withstand from in shallow hands. Black terror in the daunting hours of existence I've witnessed sinful sorrows and hopeless tomorrows standing parallel to places of ordeals with a conundrum mimicking the chaotic crescendo in my mind. A sweet deadly serum that drips from your lips I am awestruck by the gravity of your grace but hopelessly doubting my existence because, I am beginning to fade away.

In-Humane

If I ejaculated the astro-abyss from my mind, could I spill reality with seeds and create a new vision from my very own body. The sexual intensity of the climax resulting in cataclysmic crash of pleasure and pain remaining inhumane once I grasp for breath from the sin I have committed. To say it is I who has created everything from one seed will be blasphemy at the highest stage of alchemy you can create with semen formed tetra gram seals. If I could ejaculate the pain from my heart out into the open air would you feel a mixture of pleasure or pain? The fusing of sexual desire and regretful pain entering the human brain causing chaos for all of humanity.

Bookform

To even justify that existence has had a significant impact on my life is that of uncertainty, if I could I would transcend human form and turn myself into the book of the universe. Those laws and rules of stagnation that has limited me has grew grudgingly in my mind because existence knows that I am the only one who has ever surpassed existence, simply by transcending that of normal reality, it is I who had turned my skin and flesh into pages of books and suffocated myself into a deep sleep with words written on pages that can only be opened if read. Because of the idea that you can surpass existence and just not exist at the same time has baffled me in the most questionable of ways, because I usually simply ask myself, why am I bound? It is that me being boundless means I have to exist in order for my mind to come to the conclusion that I am even boundless? Or is it that I'm just caught in a paradox of simultaneously existing and not existing at the same time in the universe. Is it that the only way for me to truly exist is if I'm in book form? Or is it that I'm only nonexistent, when I'm not in book form.

Braille

You made me see a different light, with the braille on your skin when I was blinded by lust. Lusting for the skin of those who tormented my desires with distorted contorted flesh burned on empires of my mind. You covered my vision by ripping off the skin of your vision and burned it on top of mines, fusing our skin to trap my lusting desires in a binding tight rope of glorifying hopelessness that I would ever get out of this unwinding slope. Is it those ropes that tied mental strokes of desperately trying to touch something solid to recognize real reality? Or am I just trapped in the thread of existence defying laws of matter I am never seen or heard or felt, I only exist, and its only in the certain crack in the cranium of insanity that those who recognize even a stench of my existence, see that the reality I am trapped in, by lusting for her is made of only something being able to be mentally touched, and that's mental braille.

And if you're blind to the reality around you, you will never find me sweet heart, because I am trapped in lust, by mental braille.

Beloved

I've burned away at centuries of erosion to my reasons for being here. A pondered question indeed I'd sat in blissful meditation for centuries, eroding my consciousness away. Now I write these words, hoping you can understand them, as they are my last comprehensive thoughts before I reach a state of Godhood. My beloved, you are the epitome of my salvation and the channeling of my feelings into something tangible. Your demise is what called for my sudden departure of my own consciousness. A self-discovery journey who's chosen me for the long walk home. I must do it alone, my beloved, for you always held my hand and now, you can only do it in spirit, you only guide me through peaks and valleys gently grabbing that same hand and comforting me when the road gets tough. Now I come back to the crux of my paragraph to say that I am now journeying to self-discovery on this road to nirvana, and you, beloved, will always have a place in my heart.

The Demon

Suffering in the black abyss of the dark holes behind my eyes, those holes that suck reality away from my sanity I am always receding down the line of endless death. The demons that claw at my eyes I cry black tears with red eyes screaming at these words I rip out of my skin. The demon in me is trying to be freed from my soul of sorrow in hell from damnation. A poetic chain on my soul from the demonized hypnotism I received from these words that never leave my mind. As a dead poet these words claw and slice and cut through brain tissue that have me chocking on oil that burns my throat I can't scream, I can only moan. Moan at the solitary imprisonment of a deranged creation of demonic words that leave black air in the sky when I speak. Black roses, black clouds, tainted air, burning cold hell, he dwells in. He is the demon.

God's Adrift

Sitting on the adjacent possible, the possibilities of an endless slope of unwinding evaporations. I've Stood at the elevated clouds of uncertainty, that clouds distorted visions of reality unchecked by the hands of god himself, Who's godly hands hasn't seen or touched this surface unscaled by any human eye, in the connections of existence. I've been at the fore gate of a rainy revelation; the teardrops of the dead reveal sacred scriptures of my once fallen predecessors. In the absence of fate, I've sealed my deal, to be bonded with these words I write from my fingertips to the top of my skull, the formula to unlock a poet's sanctuary. Standing on the adjacent possible of an endless future, a door is revealed, the cursit words that bind and chain this locked door, a burn of black blood that drips down, forever and ever. This door opens, to an endless future, of possibilities. I've been at this gate before, standing before this door, the endless fate, of a parallel truth. I've been down this road before, standing, adjacent, on god's thumb.

The Exile

I am, from a burn of touch, heave the gravity of a poison lust clouded by a certain dead I am. Ground gravity that grabs my humanity like a lion grabbing his prey pray for the day of Black Death doomed in a sour tastefulness. I bleed a creed of a thousand mysteries of eyes that look upon me, shadows of insanity that creep up on me in the yester nights of tomorrows and forever's, being a never ending pattern of resuscitation from death and rebirth. A crushed earth and fallen heaven, dead God and buried Satan saturated the soil of red rocks that I step on. I am not from the place of lost souls and buried poets who dare challenge god himself to a deadly game of ungodly growls. I've emerged from the sanctuary of space libraries woven between time threads of galactic stardust. I am in clouded essence of dreams merged with reality blending of senses absorbing sense of self, seen on satellite monitors governed by the demons in me I am. I am, from all of the buried souls beneath ground.

Poetic Orgasm

If I could create a sound wave by the vibrations of my tongue when I speak, I'd torment the insecurities laid dormant in your mind. I'd draw parallel suns on your back that shine and intertwine through your spine so my rhymes can warm you while you walk to the divine. If I could I'd try to split the moon so each of us could have some light to light the darkness of not being by one another's side. If I could write rhymes all day and all night down your spine, my pen would stimulate your curves while my words curve on your surface, then my words make love to your energy sending your body into a sensational arouse giving you a poetic orgasm, if I could.

Skin

Exhilarating pulses that trickle down your skin as you begin to awaken from the dormant world that lies within. Senseless sense that absorbs your common sense you're under the trickling skin's common senses, sensitive to your skin the trickling of the liquid that drips down on your skin. The sensitive senses the absorbing pressure of the atmosphere that liquidates the air vapors that your vaginal tunnel leaks causing liquidation to your senses and common sense, senses because you melt all over me when my tongue touches your skin, common sense because you lose all form of sense once my tongue touches your senses. I am out of my mind when I make sense of the sexual stimulations I create when my tongue touches the commons of your senses, vibrating the verbal anomalies your skin's senses rise up fusing with me we begin to exfoliate the dead skin's common sense we begin to create, a new sense of skin.

Overdream

From the longings of companionship, to the stable-ness of the central nervous system, a poet just wants to be loved. In those dark hours of writing a black pencil is a sword piercing the heart of reality with a stained vision in mind with an artist so infatuated with the unknown. The ultimate reality you might say from a parallel universe. His pen reaches across millions of universes to create a beautiful symphony of harmony, the stroke of the pen in synchronization, vibrating at the same time as an average heartbeat.

If I could write poetry to mimic your heartbeat, the sanctuary of saturated soils buried by love, and the tormented vision enslaved by brute force of a light-bending catastrophe, I would have seen the invisible thread of time that runs through reality and stops at the center of the heart. In an obelisk I write these words hoping to touch the hearts and minds of millions of other horrid, wicked, daydreamers who suffered for their art. The deranged insane minds of data logged program computers whose system is corrupted in over dream.

Poetic Scar

Engraved in the dark spaces of black wires, the burning liquid of darkness enriched in my soil, the soul of Satan saturated in insanity solidifying in a singularity of significance. I have hoped to have reached a place of black infinity when I reach out and try to breath in the breathless existence of space, the burning stars that heat up the dark liquid of space is what keeps my blood blackened as if I was burnt by my very existence in space, sensitive sensors scarred by the sensitivity of a scar that has yet to heal. I am a walking bruise, I am a poetic scar.

Walls of Infinity

Visualizations that program mental stimulations of your mind when my energy shakes your sacred yoni, giving you mental hickeys with my words, my thrusting vocals sucking all the sanity from the base of your spine. Imagine each letter gently piercing through your spinal cord. Each letter is a vibrational shock to your vaginal walls and the beginning letter of your name is the greatest of them all, then the density of my words will make the walls of your vaginal crater cringe and release your humanity all over my mental manifestations that vibrate causing the air around us to liquidate on the walls of the room traversing matter creating its very own uterine wall. I am like a scientist studying drips of the drops your wetness falls on my mind soaking my mental visualizations of your mothership, galactic sex penetrating the inner depths of the universe through your uterus, and lastly using my imagination to capture your fantasies like a dream catcher catching your wet dreams when my words mesmerize you into a deep penetrating sleep.

Serenity

Insights of an insignificant number of sounds soaring through the sun, sitting adjacent to the symmetry of the solar universe, a manifestation of galactic expression, emptied minds and visionary eyes that pierce through space and time. And the opened doors to the unknown and journeys of reaches far beyond the horizons of reality. For this vision is twisted and torn from unearthly tether, but nonetheless is a beautiful symphony when one reaches the sun.

The Mouth of the Void

I've been buried for eons under submerged weights of existence. A theory of mines I have to surpass existence is a plague of immense torture to the psyche. Bondage of 3D reality in front of me trying so desperately to be free. Screams of horror dried up hopes of ever seeing the new horizon scraping up the bits and pieces of sanity I have left in this horrid head of mines. I write these thoughts down trying to transcend ink to reality trying to un-bind the bondage of existence placed upon me. To enter the mouth of the void, the other-side, the demons of heaven, the Angels of hell, and the gatekeepers, all in front of me, guiding me, walking with me, as I take my steps into oblivion and shed my skin into something not known to anything in the cosmos. I have untethered the sub-consciousness from all of existence and found a new since of freedom in the void from which I have entered the mouth of the void. This gate, this hole, this, existence, it drives me mad. Haunting me, telling me to enter, a slow, dark, deep, but soothing voice, telling me to enter, enter, enter the mouth of the void, and watch, you will surpass existence.

The Great Dawn

I've begin erode a sense of self from when I committed slow suicide every time I refused to write. I'd stare at a hopeless sky whose eyes drove me to slow suicide. Reciting's of the devil's harmonics an endless chatter that repeated in my mind, backwards record players that danced on two feet as they chimed in. an understanding of that which I proceeded to disassemble an idea I thought was me. An echo of immutable silence, which placed it's purging prowls on me. I stood at a place I thought was somewhere only to realize I was nowhere, nowhere in sight nor sound nor touch, not even a stench of my reality was leaking out to locate all forms of life in my vicinity. I then arose from what I now realize was an eternal slumber of consciousness I then too, was placed, by those who dare challenge god himself. They must of thought I wouldn't be able to avenge my own suicide with pencil gripped lies I told everyone please forgive me I have failed you all. I had taken my own life by submerging these words into a sleep from which they would never wake, an echo of silence so great it evaporated a sense of self from me. Now I stand adrift in this existence I look out to a parallel sun, rising from the ashes of dead poets who walked here before me, leaving behind there essence as to relay a message for me to witness, The Great Dawn.

Acknowledgements

I'd like to extend my deepest gratitude to those who have helped this book flourish. To those who have helped me along the way, and to those who have yet to join me on this galactic quest of love, freedom, beauty, and truth. A special thanks to these special people. My cousin, **Rodman Davis aka Rodddzilla**, appreciating those late night post of not only poetry, but anything that is an extension of myself and showing love and believing in me. My illustrator and relative of mines, my cousin, **Christopher Neal**, who illustrated the cover for this book. His creativity, unparalleled, and his creative vision for all of his work is absolutely astonishing. My friends and family and personal favorites who helped me on this journey.

    Lawrence Johnson, who've I've known since childhood in elementary school. Those phone conversations about the deeper parts of one's self and the universe. Your friendship and love is unbound. **Giovanni Desir**, man! This guy right here, if I tell you about this guy, I can write a book, ironic lol, but man what can I say, he's helped me a lot. All those FaceTime calls, those talks, telling me to believe in myself and that I got this, those words will forever stay in my heart, your love is limitless. **Khadijah**

Holmes. Man, those talks about a lot of stuff, believing in me, giving me guidance and setting me straight when I needed it, I will always appreciate that, your love is always there. **Affadasha Alexandria.** We haven't talked as much as we use to, but the love is still and will always be there, I'd like to thank you because you were there from the beginning, when I didn't even consider myself a poet. Those sloppy writings and spilling of thought on paper and you still believed in me, thank you always. My cousin **Tre**, for always being there just listening to what I had to say, great minds think alike, thanks man. My mom, **Sherry Anderson**, dad **Seymour Waite**, for all the unconditional love and support and the birthing of the grand poet himself. I am forever in your debt. And last but not least my aunt, **Deon Davis**, who made all of this happen, words can't express how much I appreciate you giving me this opportunity to excel in my creativity, I always knew I was good at something, I always knew I was different, and turned out it was poetry. You giving me this opportunity as you being an author is something I wouldn't of imagined. I can't thank you enough for this. A special thanks to everyone who has helped me along the way in this journey, in this galactic quest, of love, freedom, beauty, and truth from the words etched to the palms of my hands, I give you a taste of the void, inside the galactic librarian.

www.ingramcontent.com/pod-product-compliance
Lightning Source LLC
LaVergne TN
LVHW041504070426
835507LV00009B/801